Saachi the Angel

Written by
Amelie Sultana Patel and Harriet Hellen Paulk Hessam
illustrated by
Tiffany LaGrange

the PeppertreePress
www.peppertreepublishing.com

ISBN: 978-1-61493-933-7
Library of Congress:
2023922300
Printed: December 2023

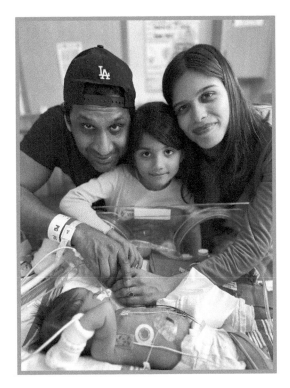

This book is dedicated to Saachi Helen Patel, Amelie's sister and Harriet's granddaughter. She was the most beautiful baby we have ever known and we miss her beyond words. But our family knows that she is with us in spirit and that she is one of God's most special angels who watches over us. We all look forward to being with her again one day. In the meantime, we see her in our dreams and visions. She comes to us as a butterfly and as a bird, and often sends us other signs that tell us she is near. We hear her laughter and feel her joy of being with our family members in heaven, especially her great-grandmother Hellen, for whom she was named.

Ravi the Raccoon and Mahaley the Meerkat lived in a forest.
They had a very large family. Their parents were monkeys, hares, cheetahs, and tigers.
Their brothers and sisters were lions, jaguars, giraffes, and skunks.
Thier nephews were squirrles, rabbits and newts.

Ravi the Raccoon and Mahaley the Meerkat had a lovely daughter, Amelie the Alpaca.
They found her when she was a poor little girl, who had no family of her own, so they
brought her to live with them in the forest.
They loved her dearly.

Livingston Lion

Jamie Jaguar

Hellen Hare

Geeta Giraffe

Champa Cheetah

Sterling Squirrel

Tawab Tiger

Vasant Vervet Monkey

Harriet Hare

Remington Rabbit

Niam Newt

Sean Skunk

3

Amelie the Alpaca and her parents had such a big
family that they couldn't fit in a house, so they all lived together
in a beautiful forest.

Amelie the Alpaca and her cousins Sterling the Squirrel, Remington
the Rabbit, and Niam the Newt enjoyed swimming in the lake to cool off.
And they liked to climb trees and swing on vines.
Amelie loved her cousins, but often wished that she had a baby sister.

Ravi the Raccoon and Mahaley the Meerkat decided to give Amelie the Alpaca a baby sister. They picked out a name for her... Saachi Helen... named her after her great-grandmother, Hellen the Hare, but they couldn't decide what kind of animal she should be. None of the choices felt quite right, so Amelie the Alpaca said "Let's wait until Saachi is born then we can decide what kind of animal she will be."

8

Everyone in the family was so excited to welcome Saachi to their forest home. They prepared a beautiful bed for her to sleep in. They brought toys for her. Everything was ready for Saachi's arrival.

Finally, after many months, Saachi Helen was born early one morning. She was the most beautiful and special baby that anyone had ever seen. But much to everyone's surprise, she wasn't an animal, and she wasn't going to get to come home with Amelie the Alpaca and her parents. Saachi Helen was so special that God decided to make her one of his angels. Amelie the Alpaca was so sad. She and her family had worked for months to prepare the baby's crib, clothes, and toys. She had made so many plans for life with a little sister. Now that Saachi had become one of God's angels, Amelie the Alpaca's dream of having a little sister seemed to be vanishing.

Amelie the Alpaca's parents saw that their daughter was very sad. That's when they told Amelie one of life's most valuable secrets: "Amelie, sometimes life takes away what we want. And we only think about what we didn't get, and that it keeps us from seeing what we got instead." Ravi the Raccoon and Mahaley the Meerkat then helped Amelie the Alpaca see things she had not yet noticed...

Trees in the forest were greener, the sun shone brighter, the birds chirped louder, more butterflies fluttered, and rainbows appeared every day. At night, thousands of stars lit up the sky. In fact, the forest had never looked so vibrant and beautiful. And it was all because of Saachi the Angel.

Amelie the Alpaca began to realize that her parents were right, that she IS a big sister. While Saachi Helen wasn't born an animal, and couldn't come home with them, she was a special gift from God. Saachi the Angel would always watch over them.

16

Amelie the Alpaca noticed all of the wonderful changes in the forest. She also felt more loved than ever before and she loved her family more than ever before. Amelie the Alpaca said to her parents, "I have the best little sister in the entire forest."

Amelie the Alpaca gathered her family around her and said,
"our lives are better because we have Saachi the Angel.
She is different from what we expected. She is our own special angel
and I am so grateful to be her big sister."
Saachi the Angel showed her family the power of love and she watches over
them every day in the forest.

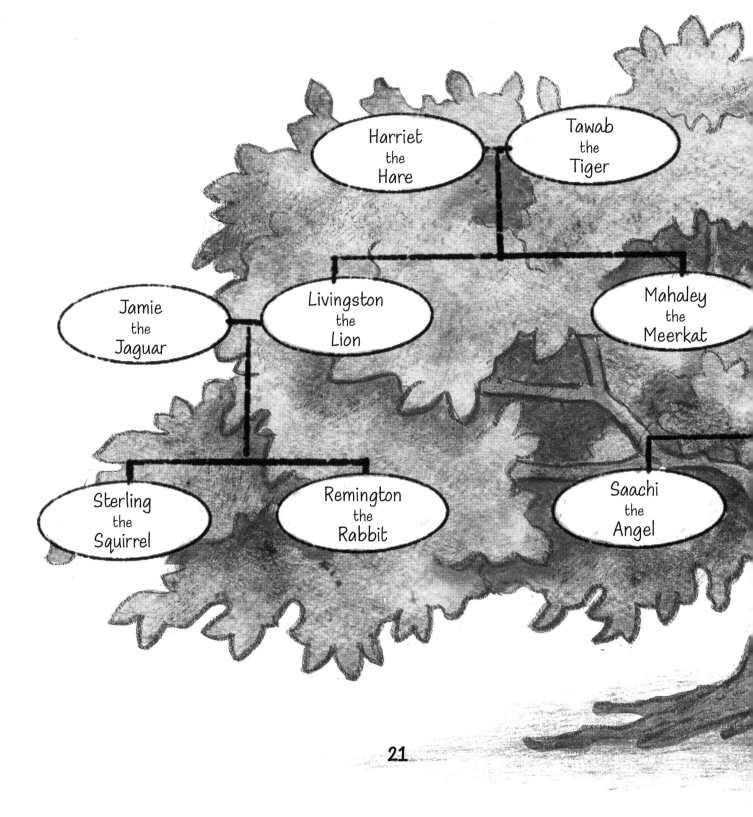

21

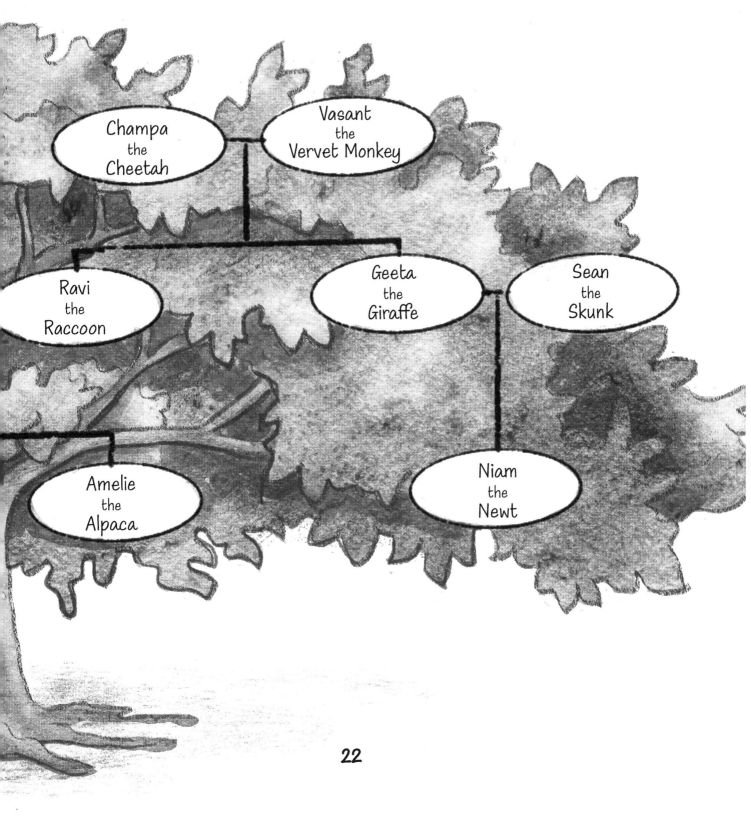

22

Printed in the USA
CPSIA information can be obtained
at www.ICGtesting.com
JSHW040756090124
54761JS00009B/6